SPLATOLOGY

and other humourous
poems to tickle your funny bone
and touch your heart.

DELLA L. DICKIE

FriesenPress

Suite 300 - 990 Fort St
Victoria, BC, Canada, V8V 3K2
www.friesenpress.com

ISBN
978-1-4602-6774-5 (Hardcover)
978-1-4602-6775-2 (Paperback)
978-1-4602-6776-9 (eBook)

1. Poetry

Distributed to the trade by The Ingram Book Company

Thank you to Marilynn Stratton for the funny poems she wrote in response to mine that contributed to the humor of this book…

Thank you to Wendy Maxwell for the formatting of my photographs. I appreciate your hard work, dear girl…

CONTENTS

WEATHERING THE SEASONS

MEMORIES

IN GOOD TASTE

FAMILY, FRIENDS AND FUN

THE CONTINUING SAGAS

GIVING THANKS

ROMANCE
AND INTRIGUE

(**Our Millarville Community Church [MCC] Writers'
Group suggested we try an 'arrow' theme.**)

CUPID SHOT HIS ARROW

Miss Ainsley and Sir Nobel
Liked each other very well,
They could see a pleasant future lay ahead.
When they started in to courting,
Sweet, dear Cupid, feeling sporting,
Shot his arrow, hitting someone else instead.

This left Sir Nobel puzzled;
No longer would she nuzzle.
Miss Ainsley was, in fact, as cold as ice.
Her manner changed completely
And she told him very sweetly
To "bug off", which he didn't think was nice.

Miss Ainsley now was taken
With the man who did the rakin'.
Yes, the gardener who kept green her big estate.
He had felt old Cupids arrow
When he bent o're his wheelbarrow
And his love for dear Miss Ainsley now was great.

Rejected for a gardener –
He wouldn't ever pardon her.
He hurried to his home to get a gun.
His anger knew no bounds,
He'd not take this lying down,
He'd put that rotten meddler on the run!

Next morning in the garden
The Gardener was up and startin'
To pick some lovely roses for his love.
Behind the shed's wood frame
Sir Nobel took his aim
To the sound of something flying up above.

When all the noise had ceased,
On the ground lay the deceased
And a stunning silence all around them grew.
It was Cupid on the ground,
His soul to heaven bound.
It seemed Sir Nobel was a poor shot too.

SAM AND SHIRLEY'S DARING ANTIC

Sam and Shirley, young romantics,
Did achieve a daring antic
To satisfy, she did insist,
An item on her Bucket List.

When a misty rain appeared
They both agreed the time was here,
Took off the clothes they were wearing;
Except for shoes, their bodies baring.

Laughing like they were insane,
They ran into the misty rain.
Childlike, hand in hand they ran,
A giggling, jiggling woman and man.

A mile they ran. Who needed sun?
No one around to see their fun
Except the cows out in the pasture.
Then the rain came down much faster.

With raindrops pelting all around
They decided then to turn around.
The breeze became a howling gale;
Thunder, lightning and oh-no! – Hail.

No place where they could get inside,
Nowhere to hide their smarting hides.
The only thing that they could do
Was to see this stupid antic through.

So back they ran, endowments flapping,
Slipping, sliding, hail stones smacking!
Yelling OUCH, and screaming pain,
She vowed they'd not do this again.

They finally reached their own front door
And in they fell upon the floor;
Battered, tattered, cold and blue.
Romance had out the window flew.

A hot bath laced with Epsom salts
Soothed their body's hail assaults.
Wrapped in bathrobes warm and dandy
They sipped on hot tea laced with brandy,

And Shirley said, "Now I can scratch
That item from my list at last!
There's nowhere now I'd rather be.
Let's brew another pot o' tea."

IKE AND AMY

I want to spin a yarn for you
A tale to tantalize
So listen as I start to pull
The wool over your eyes....

Ike and Amy Argyle
Were a homespun happy pair
They were made for each other
And they worked for a millionaire

They loved each other dearly
And were always side by side
A warm, colorful couple
Who always washed in Tide

On any Dress Occasion
They knew they were well-heeled
Ike liked to flash his diamonds
Amy's Purl-ones she revealed

They worked together side by side
As time went marching on
Until one dreadful, awful day
When Ike found Amy gone

She wasn't in the washer
Or in the dryer there
She wasn't with the other socks
Or with the underwear

Oh Amy, my dear Amy
Are you somewhere on the floor
Or clinging to a pant leg
Inside the dresser drawer

For months poor Ike was all alone
The tears he couldn't hide
His working life was over
With no partner at his side

Ike knew he'd soon be dropped inside
His boss's garbage can
Or worse, used as a cleaning rag
To keep things spic and span

Then came the day his boss reached in
And pulled Ike from the drawer
This is it, thought frightened Ike
This Argyle is no more

"Ah ha!" exclaimed the millionaire
"This really is a hoot!
I found the other one of you
Stuffed inside a boot"

And there she was, his Amy dear
Somewhat worse for wear
And Ike's poor heart was mended
For once more they were a pair

("Black Bart is one of our 'yard cowboys' made by Al from railroad spikes and painted by me. I noticed one day that a young Hawk had landed on Black Bart's hat, so I took the photo and wrote this poem.")

THE BALLAD OF BLACK BART

I came into town on a Greyhound
(Though most folks ride in on a horse)
I'm here to put cards on the table
With a Dickie's-Dive Dealer, of course.

I've got a Colt 45's in my holster
Hangin' low on my skinny black hips.
I've got looks, I've got style and I'm charming,
From my thin lips the honey just drips.

But it seems that misfortune has found me.
My ego balloon has gone flat.
I was strutting along out on Main Street
When a bird landed right on my hat!

Now I can't be the card-shark I portray,
No one takes me seriously.
And what's worse, this bird seems to like me
Or it thinks I'm a Black Forest tree

I'm not Number One with the ladies
With Number Two on my Cravat.
How can I wink and look sexy
With this big fluffy bird on my hat?

I can't make a buck playing poker,
Others snicker like immature brats.
They claim I have misplaced my pecker
And now I can pee from my hat.

The Sheriff in town doesn't like me
He claims I'm a cheat and a turd.
There'll soon be a duel out on Main Street;
If I duck fast… he might hit the bird.

If I'm quicker of hand than the lawman,
There'll be nothing but trouble I'll see,
So I'm gonna leave town in the morning,
The Greyhound, the Big Bird. ..and me.

IT

If you could see what I just saw, you'd be amazed, you'd stand in awe
Your nerves would be completely raw if you had seen what I just saw!

I went outside this evening to take a little jog
In the cold and misty rain, and the thick and eerie fog.
When IT appeared before me, I froze up in surprise,
My vision's 20/20 but I disbelieved my eyes.

IT wafted there before me, so silent and so still;
My insides were a-quivering, I thought that I'd be ill.
My knees were knock-knock-knocking; it really was a shock.
I tried to run away from IT, but I couldn't even walk!

Neither could I shout for help, my throat had turned to dust.
I felt just like the tin man whose armour turned to rust.
My heart was beating way too fast; I've never felt so weird,
And just as quick as anything…IT up and disappeared!

I see you don't believe me. I know what you are thinkin',
I swear I'm being truthful, that I haven't been out drinkin',
But buddy, I'm in awful shape and I sure could use a sip.
If you could see what I just saw, you'd join me in a nip!

A STORY FOR THE LIGHT-HEARTED

There once was a young girl
All sweetness and light
Who fell for a scoundrel
Blacker than night

She was slightly light-headed
(As light as a feather)
He promised that always
They would be together

He told her that soon
They two would be wedded
So she gave him the green light
And the two became bedded

In the cold light of day
That scoundrel had gone
He had taken her money
And lit-out for Tucson

She now saw the light
She hadn't been smart
And a lighter purse makes
For a much heavy heart

How could she cope
With this heartbreak and shame
The Red-Light District
Was calling her name

She certainly needed a
Bright guiding light
Or a white Knight in Armor
Shining so bright

And lo and behold!
This Knight did appear
He gave her a job
Selling light-beer

Being light-footed
She soon climbed the ladder
Great management skills
That made her much gladder

She is now CEO
As sharp as a knife
Her Knight became husband
A bright light in her life

And In light of all this
There's nothing more graphic
Than to see she and her Knight
Trip that old Light Fantastic.

GRUMBLES
AND GRIEVANCES

THE OLD COTTON POPLAR

Spring has sprung, the grass is green
That Cotton Poplar is obscene!
It's spitting stickies everywhere;
They're on our shoes and in our hair,
And after leaves start to unfurl
From deep within will rise 'the Squirrel'
With young ones seven...maybe eight
Whom we will not appreciate!
Soon after this phenomenon....
A fluffy blanket for our lawn.
Bags of cotton we will rake
As anti-histamines we take.
The Town will soon remove this tree
And will we miss it? Probably.

DISRESPECTFUL TERMS FOR SENIORS

Antique, fossilized,
Time worn, Grey
Obsolete, Out of date
Relic, Passé

Decrepit, Seasoned
Ripened, Mature,
White-haired, Grey-haired
Out to Pasture

Old fogey, Grizzled
Ancient, Old hat
Fuddy-duddy, Used up
Gaffer, Old bat

Priggish, Persnickety,
Baldy, Old poop
Over the hill, Feeble
Fuss-budget, Stupe

Codger, Stodgy
Archaic, Old-maid
Stiff-necked, Worn out
Feeble, Decayed

Getting on, Aged
Worn-out, Oldie
Not getting younger
Pre-historic, Moldy

Out-moded, Battle-axe
Rinky-dink, Moss-grown
Old-fangled, Out of date
Extinct, Old crone

My absolute favourite
From all I've comprised...
Oh, How I love it!
It's "Methusalized"!

HOW TO TRIM A TREE WHEN YOU ARE SEVENTY-EIGHT YEARS OLD

Take two decaying two-by-fours
(Completely rotten fencing boards),
Space them out on two saw horses
Then start to defy gravity forces.

Place a ladder on the boards.
Step up then with a trimming sword
And though things seem to shake a little,
Climb way, way up into the middle.

Keep on climbing even higher
To trim the tree limbs round the wires.
Now reach up with the trimming tool,
While down below there stands a fool:

A wife, not willing, but she's ready
To hold the bloody ladder steady!
Should everything come tumbling down,
He'll take her out as he hits the ground!

STICK IN THE MUD

They call me an old stick-in-the-mud
And they try hard to convert me;
Sticks and stones may break my bones
But names will never hurt me!
My business is my business
And I really must declare,
That though they stick together
They should stick their noses elsewhere!
They offer me the short end of
That old proverbial stick,
And it sticks right in my craw
Till it darn well make me sick.
Well it sticks out like a sore thumb
That I don't stick out my neck.
They stick their noses in the air
And I think "what the heck"!
It's a sticky situation --
More than I can shake a stick at
But sticking to the facts, I say,
I'm not their lowly doormat!
Although I'd like to tell them all
Exactly where to stick it,
That's not a Christian attitude
So I'll take the wound and lick it.
I'll keep on sticking to my guns;
I'm sure that I'll live through it.
Thanks for listening - that's my story
And I'm sticking to it.

SPLATOLOGY

In springtime and in summer, as we drive around each day,
our windshields will encounter many bugs along the way.

Mosquitos of the female sort will make a little **TICK**
and leave a little red spot, not too greasy or too thick.

Now and then a bumble bee will make an awful **WHACK**
making one big yellow smear with bits of legs intact.

Then a gorgeous butterfly, with wings like silken butter
becomes a smudge of creamy goo with wings still all a-flutter.

It's amazing how those dragonflies can make a kind of **CLUNK**
and those skinny little bodies then become a trail of gunk!

I think the worst are grasshoppers; they really make a **SPLAT**
and smear across the windshield in revenge for the attack.

Sometimes I really wonder, and it really is a riddle,
why the biggest, fattest bug of all will land right in the middle.

No use in getting all up tight, it's something we must shrug off.
Just stop the car, get out your rag, and squirt a load of Bug-Off.

OOPS

BAD MEMORY, BAD EYESIGHT, OR BOTH?

We got up quite early this windy spring morn;
Clouds moving in, there might be a storm.
We showered and shaved, had a quick bite,
Dressed in our finest, an unusual sight,
Then hopped in the van at the appropriate hour
And drove into Calgary during morning rush hour.
As our timed destination was getting quite near,
No complaint, not at all, from us could you hear.
Excited to witness a wonderful sight,
We could hardly contain our joy and delight.
But lo and behold, could this be our fate?
The Parking Lot fellow wouldn't open the gate!
"You had better check further to make it all clear
Cause there's no such event going on here!"
So I phoned our dear Graduate to hear what she'd say;
"Oh Gran, this is April. My Grad's not till May".
So somewhat embarrassed we furthermore roamed
By turning around and heading back home.

INATTENTION

Being a good wife, I washed out the dirt,
Then set up the ironing board to iron a shirt,
The regular Sunday morning routine
Before going to church all pressed and clean.
I plugged in the iron (or so I had thought)
And waited until I knew it was hot.
After the shirt on the board I had spread,
I reached for the iron… got the Mixer instead.
I thought to myself "I should be more alert
But you just can't beat ironing a shirt"

TROUBLE COMES IN THREES

I have a little tale to tell that might give you a chuckle,
Yesterday we trimmed our Christmas tree.
Our house was warm and cozy – a good day for a stew
For outside it was minus thirty-three.

To accompany this hearty meal, I baked some biscuits brown
And Al and I sat down to eat our quota.
One bite of biscuit and I screamed "Oh no! It just can't be!"
Instead of baking powder I'd used soda!

We didn't like the salty taste so dumped them in the garbage
And we spent all evening after with the farts,
But we awoke this morning feeling good and energized,
A good day, I professed, for making tarts.

The pasty rolled out beautifully, in the mincemeat there was rum,
So I popped them in the oven (what a baker!)
And while they were a-baking, I moved my cactus plant
To a top shelf to make room for Christmas décor.

I don't know how it happened but that plant pot did a flip
And came down upon the carpet with a thud!
There was cactus here and cactus there and dirt just everywhere,
So I started cleaning up that awful crud!

My poor wee cactus looked so sad. I told it I was sorry,
Then I vacuumed everything so very well.
Then I had an awful thought, I didn't hear the buzzer…
From the kitchen there arose an awful smell.

My mincemeat tarts were more than brown, my language wasn't
nice!
Then I had a great idea (Oh, So Sweet!)
I dumped them in the garbage too and headed out the door
To the Bakery where I bought my Christmas treats.

RESPONSE FROM MY FRIEND, MARILYNN STRATTON

Of your misfortunes
I'm sorry to hear,
But I see that you've turned them
To humour and cheer!

True poets must suffer
And live with their curses,
Otherwise they'd have nothing
To say in their verses.

And it could have been worse;
At the whim of fate-fickle,
You might have sat down
On a cactus prickle.

So consider it lucky
That burnt tarts and gas
Were all that you suffered
And those, too, shall pass.

A TALE OF SOME BROKEN BONES

Jim rode out on a warm spring day
On the new horse he'd got for a deal
Through some mishap, poor Jim limped on home
With eight broken bones in his heel

And Jody suggested, "Sell that damn horse
He wasn't *that* good of a deal!"
But Jim refused and stayed at home
To heal up the bones in his heel.

He was on the mend but the urge was strong;
He had to climb back on that horse,
And into the forest they jaunted along
(Without his rifle, of course).

It was quiet and peaceful and Jim was at ease,
Mother Nature was giving her best,
When all of a sudden they came on a bear
Who put an end to his rest!

The big black bear didn't like the surprise
And he rose up on hind legs and roared!
Jim gave a yell and tried to encourage
His horse to rush forcefully forward.

In less than a second his horse gave a buck
And Jim met the ground with a whack.
His horse galloped off in a frenzy of fear
And never, no never, looked back.

So what have we now? A man on the ground
No rifle, no horse, what a victim!
Jim realized that the danger was high
'Cause he'd re-break his foot if he kicked him.

But the bear gave a chuckle, then ambled away
To look for more berries to eat.
Lucky ! This was a vegetarian bear
Who really was not into meat!

And Jody insisted "Sell that damn horse
His bad habits are really a sin!"
Jim had to agree and stayed home again
To heal up the break in his shin.

QUICK! GRAB THE CAMERA!

I glanced out the window and to my surprise
An unusual sight greeted my eyes;
Two white rabbits were resting that day,
Sleepy and still on the neighbour's driveway.
I ran for my camera with speed and delight
To capture the scene, ere they hop out of sight.
Dogs, cats and birds, squirrels and mule deer
Are a regular sight in the neighborhood here,
But rabbits are rare, in fact, never seen
So I wanted to capture this sight so serene.
I quietly opened and snuck out the door,
Raised up my camera then noticed with horror
A neighbour, who walks her dogs as a habit,
Is walking those dogs quite close to the rabbits.
I frantically signal – Stay back! – Stay away!
She looks at me oddly but stops anyway.
I take a quick picture, then end the suspense;
"Look at the rabbits there by the fence."
She looks at the rabbits, then calls out to me
"Two white garbage bags are all I can see"
Well, now I'm embarrassed, turn totally red
But had to laugh too, as I'm shaking my head.
Doubled over with laughter, my neighbour did say,
"Oh, Della, thank you! You have just made my day."

WILD AND TAME

THE BEAR FACTS

I'll tell you my interpretation
Of a 'happening here (with animation);
A Black Bear wandered into town
Just to have a look around.

Past the Lodge and down the hill –
He strolled past Koop's - things were still,
Then down the alley west he ambled
When someone yelled and someone scrambled...

"Look out! Look out! There is a Bear!"
Soon there were police cars everywhere
With honking horns and lights a-blazing.
People gathered. It was amazing!"

A policeman shouted good and loud
To all the "cameras" gathered round,
"Keep back!! Way back! It's not a zoo!
Bears run faster, friends, than you!"

Poor bear, as frightened as could be,
Climbed over a fence and up a tree
And hung there watching all the fuss.
We looked at him – he looked at us.

He didn't like the scene below.
He'd had enough and tried to go.
Down that tree he came so fast
But sirens screamed and horns did blast!

All his efforts were in vain,
So up the tree he climbed again.
The Wildlife Officers appeared
And had to dart the poor bear's rear.

Still further up climbed Mr. Bear
And for a long time lingered there.
One more dart, bear started down...
And soon, just tumbled to the ground.

It took four men to lift with care
That limp and furry, sleeping bear.
I'll tell you now, you needn't ask us –
They took him to the Kananaskis!

Someday, perhaps, this big old male
Will father cubs and tell this tale.
He'll warn them "Don't you go to Town
'Cause it ain't worth the look around!"

ELSA THE CAT

Your cat is not a stupid cat
Elsa knows just where it's at
She loves to purr and likes a pat
Ignores the charms of an old tomcat
No longer can your cat begat
She cannot give a tit for tat
She's not too thin and not too fat
Her fur is sleek without a matt
Her neck displays a white cravat
Sometimes she'll play and be a brat
She'll even act like a big wildcat
But she's mostly made of a sweet format
She'll sit in a box (if you take out the hat)
Or lie in the sun on the front doormat
And stretch out till she's nice and flat
Then meow for food then chase a rat
Or bat a bug till it goes splat
This is enough of this silly chitchat

GEESE

Goosey Goosey Gander
Where do we wander?
Golf course, farmer's field
Anywhere we want to!
We're in the grass, we're on the walk,
We're in the fields of harvest stock
We're on the streams, we're on the lakes
The river banks we overtake.
Although we like the rural views,
We've learned to like the city too.
You'll know when we have been around,
A slimy mess is on the ground.
You once thought geese would not exist
And put us on the endangered list;
No predators (not even man!),
So we utilized your human plan.
Thank you, folks, we're doing well.
We make your parks a living hell,
We nest in fields, on roofs, in trees
And do exactly as we please.
We guard our offspring with great care -
Try and stop us if you dare -
You'll run into an angry goose
And it will tear your clothing loose!
We peck with beak and smack with wings,
Attack your knees and other things!
Our numbers grow and reproduce,
You might say, humans have been "goosed"!

BIOLOGY OPINION

The great herds of Elk that are seen around here
Make Ranchers and Farmers quite angry, I fear.
Elk charge through the fences and eat lots of hay
That the Ranchers and Farmers have stockpiled away
To feed their own livestock during winter's long season.
Ranchers cuss and complain and Elk are the reason.

Now, Deer can jump over a fence or go under.
They too, munch on hay (with no grass, it's no wonder!).
These lovely, wild animals more damage can do
Cause they jump on the bales and poop on them too.
So come hunting season the ranchers don't wait;
They'd rather see wild meat served on a plate.

Now, Reindeer and Caribou are one and the same,
But Reindeer are Caribou beasts that are tamed.
Santa has eight of these reindeer,…no nine!
He couldn't use Elk; that would be a crime!
They would charge through the fences with Santa and sleigh
And scatter those millions of toys on the way.

Then you see, the dear children all over this land
Would be crying and certainly would not understand
That Santa, dear Santa, was caught in barbed-wire,
His sleigh is a wreck and no longer a 'flyer',
His Elk team got free from the harness and fled,
And no toys were a-waiting when they climbed out of bed.

To summarize quickly your question, "I've found
I am the only Elk lover around!"

DOWN DEEP AND DIRTY GOPHER BLUES

One warm, sunny day my sister ran off
To explore the world near the highway;
Unaware of the sound, a truck brought her down.
That was a week ago Friday.
It was Papa that found my poor little Sis,
Imagine our shock at the news;
She was longer and wider with nothing inside her
And I've got those Gopher blues.

(I've got those down deep and dirty Gopher blues)

My dear Uncle Gomer whistled his songs
As we played in the sun 'round our den.
He'd stand straight and proud, and whistle out loud
Now his whistling has come to an end.
He didn't look up when the shadow appeared,
He struggled but couldn't get loose.
I have a hunch he was eaten for lunch
And I've got those Gopher blues.

(I've got those down deep and dirty Gopher blues)

It's a hard life out here on the prairie.
The dangers we face are horrific.
Our species we fear, might soon disappear
That's why we are so damn prolific.
We struggle to keep our heads above ground,
We deal with such hate and abuse;
To kill us or eat us is no way to treat us,
And I've got those Gopher blues

(I've got those down deep and dirty Gopher blues)

COWHAND AND COYOTE

One day when I was mendin' fence
Somethin' caught my eye.
I saw a big ol' coyote
Slowly saunterin' by.

I looked at him, he looked at me,
I said "How do you do?"
He paused for just a moment
Then he said "Just fine... and you?"

Well, dang it, I was speechless,
For it's a well-known fact
That coyotes never say a word.
This one had answered back!

He looked at me quite strangely,
Then slowly trotted on.
As I sat there on my haunches,
I finally said "Dog gone!"

Had I really heard that coyote talk?
Things seemed kinda hazy...
If I ever tried to tell someone
They'd think that I'd gone crazy

Right then I started wondering
'Perhaps I'd had a "spell"
Or maybe I *was* crazy –
That was possible as well.

Maybe spending too much time
With no one else but me;
Can't wag the jaw all by myself.
I must need company.

So I got back to mendin' fence.
What happened I can't explain,
But should that coyote amble by
I'm gonna ask… "Think it'll rain?"

BLUEBIRD

How can he hide? What can he do?
Nothing can camouflage radiant blue.
Soon leaves on the trees will provide him some cover
Till then, he'll be followed by this bluebird lover.
How can he hide? What can he do?
Just flitter and flutter from my camera's view.
He finds a fine box, just right for a nest
And waits for his mate to agree to invest
Her time and her talent to build an abode
They can share, for the season, by the side of the road.
When their nest has been feathered, eggs she will lay;
While she's sitting on eggs, he'll keep trouble away.
He's fast, fierce and feisty; and this I applaud.
I'm always so grateful for this blue-gift from God.

WEATHERING

THE SEASONS

SPRING'S PROMISE

Spring shows her promise
There's melting of snow
And signs of her beauty
Wherever we go

Owls in their nests
Geese here and there
Swans on the pond
Ducks in the air

The sky is true blue
Clouds gather and fly
Changing their shapes
As they quickly fly by

Gophers are playing
On snow – leap and bound
The Hawks and Eagles
Are hovering around

And there on a fence post
A wonderful sight
A beautiful Bluebird
My springtime delight

SNOW ARTIST (HAIKU)

snow artist at work
howling wind, fresh heavy snow
drift-sculpting begins.

BENEATH MY BIG UMBRELLA

If you should wander down the street
As rain is pouring down,
And you open your umbrella
With a whooshy-snappy sound,
Should you ignore the others
Who are scurrying all around
To find some shelter from the rain
As it bounces on the ground?

One day the rain began to pour
My mood was very mellow.
I offered to share my waterless space
With a most extraordinary fella;
I found out he was a singer
So we sang A Capella
All the way to work that day
Beneath my big umbrella.

She was waiting at the bus stop
Getting wetter by the second,
But jumped right in beside me
When I smiled at her and beckoned,
And we shared our own dry humour
'Til the bus came and she stepped on.
My kind and sharing gesture caused
A real nice time, I reckoned!

I think we should remember that
There's room for more than one.
Beneath a big umbrella
You can have a lot of fun!
By sharing with another
You can walk instead of run.
When you're keeping dry together
You just don't miss the sun!

CHINOOK (HAIKU)

arch of ragged cloud
a streaked eyelash in the sky
blue pupil staring

CLOUDS

Clouds fly high across the sky, to chase an unknown foe.
Streaks of light against the blue of autumn sky they flow.
My thoughts fly too and soon my spirit soars up wild and free,
Riding high upon the racing clouds in ecstasy.

Winter skies of leaden grey, shut out the warming sun,
Looming low and sullen too, move slowly on and on;
Formless clouds that bear down on my helpless state of mind
Producing total dullness and to weariness resigned.

Then come the wondrous clouds of spring, they feather, shift and curl.,
In the stunning April sky they flow, take shape and swirl
Then they darken, threaten rain, they rumble and they roar.
I hold my face up to the sky; excited, wanting more.

My summer skies are beautiful; clouds so fluffy white
Float across the deep blue sky, a most delightful sight.
I lay down on the fragrant grass and watch them drift and play
And I'm as peaceful as the sky. I love those summer days.

The seasons come, the seasons go, and clouds reflect my mood.
I need a blue sky, wind and clouds or else I sit and brood.
I am a woman, Alberta born, who knows a sunny sky
Will lift my spirit like the wind and with the clouds I'll fly.

WINTER IN ALBERTA

When snow goes CRUNCH beneath your boots
When equipment balks at being started,
When sky and earth are frosty gray
And everyone feels down-hearted.

When temperatures are minus 30
With winds that make the wind-chill scary,
And backs are sore from shoveling
Those sidewalks that are buried.

When frost fills up your window view
And the walls give off a draft;
Our heating bills are all that's 'up'.
Why are we here? We must be daft!

But then… the sun begins to shine
And the mercury starts to rise;
Sun on snow is beautiful,
A visual feast before our eyes

Frosted trees and glistening snow
Like diamonds cast upon the white;
The sky becomes a brilliant blue
And our world, it seems, is quite alright.

THISTLE DOWN

The down of thistle
Awaiting the wind
To scatter the seed
So new growth begins

MAKING EXCUSES

Snow is a-falling, the temperature too;
I'm here in my warm house with little to do.
It's too cold to walk, too slippery to drive.
I'll curl up with a book cause it's comfy inside;
But my conscience - it bugs me, gets under my skin,
Saying, "Move it before *rigor mortis* sets in".

I put on the layers of clothing I need:
Start with the woolies and then I proceed
With flannelette pj's crushed under my jeans,
A sweatshirt, a vest, with a sweater between.
My boots, with two pairs of socks, barely fit,
Now on with my jacket, my toque, scarf & mitts.

I waddle outside like a brave pioneer,
Start walking along and feel glad to be here.
Now that I am moving, my body feels good
Allowing my muscles to do what they should.
It's quiet and peaceful, no one have I met;
They're all inside (making excuses, I bet.)

MEMORIES

HE NEVER RODE A BUCKING BRONC

(a song for my father, James Frederick Maxwell)

Jim was just a city boy raised down in the Hat
There he met his Helen, one look and that was that.
Her father, Charlie Mickle, was there for a year or more
Rounding up wild horses back in nineteen-twenty-four.
Jim found a job with Calgary Power in a town they called Seebe,
He and Helen settled there and had children, one, two three.
Charlie Mickle's cowboy friends often came to call,
About that time Jim met Pete Knight, the greatest of them all.

In nineteen-thirty-seven, they were moved to Calgary.
Another child was born to them (and I'm glad that it was me).
In 'forty-six, the Cowboys' Protective Association
Offered him a part time job (with full-time dedication).
As Secretary/Treasurer, he can well remember,
There were only 15 rodeos and just one hundred members.
He helped to advertise events on both sides of the border,
Jim worked with the Management and kept the books in order.

By the year of nineteen-sixty-three, the membership had grown;
There were five-hundred cowboys and over fifty rodeos.
Jim simplified the system with a Rodeo Directory
Where prizes, fees, and rodeo dates were there for all to see.
When the work-load got too heavy, he could hardly keep the pace,
He decided to retire -- two full-timers took his place.
The Cowboys paid him tribute, they honoured his good name
By voting him a Member of the Cowboy Hall of Fame.

He never rode a bucking bronc, he never roped a steer
But he sure helped the Cowboys for over sixteen years.
A dedicated Builder, Jim Maxwell is his name.
His picture now is hanging in the Cowboy's Hall of Fame.

(The Canadian Rodeo Cowboy Hall of Fame).

HELEN NORIENNE (MAXWELL) GROVER

(my dear sister)

We didn't live together long –
Thirteen years, that was all,
Before she married, moved away
But many memories I recall

When I was oh so very young
She read my childhood books to me:
Alice in Wonderland, Winnie the Pooh,
And A.A. Milne's poetry.

She made those stories very real.
I knew each character by heart.
She gave my life-long love of books
A very healthy, happy start.

She also loved to sing to me
And one time it was quite absurd,
We both cried as she sang "Old Shep".
It was the best song that I'd ever heard!

When I wrote my childish poems
Or had to sing before a crowd,
Her warm encouragement and praise
Always made me feel so proud.

Then she met Ed and fell in love
And soon it was their wedding day.
Though our bedroom was now all mine,
I missed her when she moved away.

But I didn't really know Norienne
As one woman to another.
When she left home I was a kid,
She was like my second mother.

Her life was there, mine was here;
We had short visits in between.
Our kids were babies, boys, then men
Almost overnight, it seems.

Last fall when she was very ill
I had some precious weeks down there.
Her days were all an up-hill climb
But we got to share what sisters share.

I thank our God I had that chance
To be with her, to laugh and cry;
To share things deep within our hearts.
How hard it was to say goodbye.

My sister was a gentle soul
A lady always, through and through,
Sweet and loving, always kind
And she fought her battle bravely too.

LITTLE COUSIN OF MINE

(*in memory of cousin Gayle Loblaw-Vipond*)

I remember those days on the old Bottrel farm
In the summer, when we were just kids.
I remember the sights and all of the sounds
I remember the things that we did.
We used to play hide-n-go-seek in the barn
Till a mouse started chewing my hair.
We giggled a lot, there was so much to do,
There was never a moment to spare.

Wild flowers and strawberries covered the hill.
I loved those big trees down the lane.
The squeak and the slam of that old farmhouse door
And the lullaby sound of the rain,
The shade of the woods and the old swimming hole,
A breakfast of trout from the stream.
We walked to the old General Store in the sun
For those popsicles, cold as a dream.

We told dirty jokes and we talked about boys,
And all of our secrets we shared.
In the black of the night, in the bunkhouse alone,
I'd tell ghost stories till you were scared.
I envied the way you could jump on a horse
Cause I needed a boost every time.
I still see you prancing that old Dixie mare
While Shorty and I trudge behind.

Little cousin of mine, how the years have flown by
Since the country and city girls shared summertime
I've carried with me all those good memories
And I thank you, little cousin of mine.

A MICKLE FAMILY PHOTOGRAPH

(*Relatives on my Mother's side*)

There's a picture on my wall, quite worn from all the looking,
Grandpa Charlie Mickle's birthday celebration.
All seven of his children and their spouses all together
And in front, their kids (the Younger Generation).

I guess the date would be about 1944
And I'm sitting with my cousins on the ground.
I didn't know back then how much each one would mean to me,
Or the special times I'd have with them around.

Like the time at Auntie Rita's, when I jumped at my big chance
To ride behind my cousin Garry on a horse.
We went to get the milk cows and he ducked to miss a branch
That dumped me off! An accident, of course.

Or when I stayed with Cousin Gayle, and one night they let us sleep
Out in the bunkhouse by ourselves, and we were brave,
Till Jack and Ted got on the roof and howled like souls possessed
And sent us screaming to the house where we'd be safe.

I have so many stories of my childhood's summer fun
And reunions that enriched the ties that bind.
Many of my cousins were called away too soon
But their memories in my heart forever shine.

Each aunt of mine was special, always kind and full of fun
And all my uncles were my heroes and my friends,
Though at times they were as crazy as a bunch of loony-tunes,
They all had my respect right to the end.

They're gone, those special people, like my own dear mom and dad
And the numbers of first-cousins now are few,

But second cousins, and the thirds, and cousins once-removed
Are spreading out, and up and down, and over too.

As I gaze now at the picture of the Mickle's way back then
It creates in me a very weird sensation,
To realize that time has taken me from then to now
And I'm a member of the Older Generation!

So at the next reunion, share the memories and the love
Share our stories with the young ones – have a ball!
And line up for a picture – stand together and be proud
Of the Mickle blood that's flowing through us all.

IN GOOD TASTE

HOME-MADE BREAD

(for Jean and the tasty bread she makes)

There's nothing like the taste of home-made bread.
It just pleasures both the nose and taste buds too;
A peanut butter sandwich with a big, cold glass of milk,
Or a huge slice thickly buttered with beef stew.

I love it lightly toasted beneath my scrambled eggs,
Or sprinkled with brown sugar and some cinnamon.
It always seems to be, that in no-time-flat,
Where once there was a loaf, now there is none.

I just cannot imagine ever tiring of the taste,
It is something that I really do enjoy.
But if I should consume home-made bread every day
I'd look just like the Pillsbury Dough Boy!

RABBIT STEW FOR BRENDA

Ol' Granny lounged there on the deck
A drink in one hand (what the heck!)
In the other, a bee-bee gun...
She was going to have a little fun!
There she sat, just a-waitin'
Smilin' and anticipatin';
Soon those little rascal rabbits
Will hop on in (as is their habit)
To eat her tender garden veggies
Which makes ol' Granny more than edgy.
When those bunnies start to nibble
A bee-bee blast right through their middle
Will end this garden thievery
And there'll be stew for you and me!

TIME TO HARVEST

Be grateful for the garden;
Just look at that sight,
Abounding with veggies
All colours, all ripe.
You've coaxed and you've coddled,
You've watered with care,
Now all you have sowed
Is awaiting you there.

It's now time to harvest;
You pull them with ease,
You wash and you bag,
You can and you freeze,
You pickle, you bake,
No time for martinis.
You ask the big question,
Why did I plant zucchinis?

They grow to be giants;
You cake 'em, you bake 'em.
You still have a mountain
Nobody will take 'em.
You give away loafs,
You give away pickles,
If only those zucchinis
Were down to a trickle.

But more monsters a-wait
So you grind some more relish,
And still there are more.
This harvest is hellish!
So remember next year,
Don't plant those nightmares.
Just wait, because someone
Will offer you theirs.

ONCE UPON A CAKE PLATE

A long time ago in a place called Temptation
There stood a white angel so frosty and light,
Covered with strawberries, bright red and juicy;
A beautiful, eye-catching, tea-time delight.

She beckoned so sweetly to me as I passed her
And she called out to me, with an elegant flair,
"Come, try my delicate happy-mouth flavour",
While wafting her fruity-cream scent here and there.

But just further on something else caught my eye…
A big chocolate two-layered beast of a cake
And topping it off -- a chocolate fudge frosting
With an aroma that told me it wasn't a fake!

It sat there and looked me right straight in the eye
And it said, *"There's more fudge in-between.
You know if you put a big piece on your plate,
You could top it all off with ice-cream"*!

Oh, which one of these two should a weak person choose?
They both seem to tempt me with ease…
The hostess is waiting. I must make a choice…
"A big piece of both, if you please."

SWEET ADDICTION

(a Valentine coffee theme from the Poetry Group)

I admit to loving coffee.
I can't start the day without it.
A cup of tea at midday
Picks me up, no doubt about it!

A glass of wine pre-dinnertime
Makes me hungry for the food.
A mug of sweet, hot chocolate
Puts me in a happy mood.

These things are not a problem,
Except where weight is concerned.
Bad habit, not addiction,
Is what I have discerned.

I do have one addiction though,
I need it all the time.
Don't want to do without it.
That's Al, my Valentine.

A POEM FOR WENDY

(my little niece)

I'm writing this small poem to you
Who has the same affliction;
It must run in our family
This… chocolate addiction!

Last night before the Idol show
I had an awful craving.
I made a pan of chocolate fudge
So good, we both were raving.

The watching and the waiting for
Our Idol to perform
Caused me to get so jittery
My body got too warm.

I had to munch on something!
The fudge was close at hand.
It satisfied my craving but
The outcome wasn't planned…

Our idol didn't do as well as
She had done before
So I ate another piece of fudge
And then, I ate some more.

Before I hit the sack last night
The pan was almost gone,
And I, upon this sugar 'high',
Lay wide-awake till dawn.

I ask you, little niece of mine,
   To sympathize with me.
   I get no sympathy at all
From 'he' who lives with me.

   You are the only family who
      I have come upon,
Who'll make a great big pan of fudge
      And pick it till it's gone!

   I am in fear of weeks to come
      For the "Idol" I must see,
   And if I keep on eating fudge
There'll be much-too-much of ME!

REED'S DAY OF FISHING

(inspired by Reed Dickie's story)

Reed Dickie and friend set out to go a-fishin' one fine day.
They stopped to fill the truck with gas and went inside to pay.
When the Philippian cashier heard what they were doing to do,
She said, "Please save the fish's head so I can make some stew".

On the lake they stopped the boat and both did cast their lines.
The sun was warm, the beer was cold and they were feelin' fine.
What better hobby could there be than floating on the blue?
It was a bright spring morning, nothing better could they do!

It wasn't long before Reed felt a great tug on his line.
He knew he'd hooked a big one and he'd have to fight this time.
Fight he did before he finally pulled it up and in;
A Giant Pike! A Monster Fish! A Fishing Trophy Win!

The size of that big monster Pike made them hoot and laugh.
They measured that big fish and it was 3 feet and a half.
When they put it on the scale it weighed over 18 pounds,
One of the biggest catches folks had made for miles around.

That fish turned out to be the only fish they caught that day,
So they went ashore, hooked up the boat, and went upon their
way.
A brief stop at the gas bar; Reed remembered a request.
He walked up to the Cashier who was busy at a desk.

"You asked me if I caught a fish, its head to you I'd bring.
Sister, you can have it. In fact, take the whole darn thing!"
When he held the fish aloft her chin dropped to the floor,
And when she stewed that fish up she had soup forevermore.

(This poem composed itself after one of the wonderful musical jams we've had over the years with our special group of "Friends".)

WILD RICE MUSHROOM GRAVY

We looked forward to the evening; dinner and a Jam
With a group of super folks that we call friends.
Oh, the hors d'oeuvres were delicious, the dinner was divine,
But the atmosphere went wonky about then.

A severe case of the giggles spread itself around the room
And too soon became those howling gales of laughter.
Though the music really sounded quite acoustic to the ear,
Everyone was quite electrified thereafter.

The banjo played much faster and the fiddle was on fire,
And each picker played the best they've ever played!
The vocals were pure Nashville with exquisite harmony;
You would almost think that we were getting paid.

Could it have been the tasty, icy fruit punch?
Or the herbs and spices in the brown bread maybe?
It might have been the sweet and luscious pork chops,
But we suspect it was the Wild Rice Mushroom Gravy.

FAMILY,
FRIENDS AND FUN

(a letter-poem to my brother, Charles T. Maxwell)

DEAR CHUCK,

In response to your recent letter
Teaching mail delivery history
And the etiquette of letter writing
So it no longer is a mystery,
I send to you a 'thank you, sir'
For all the information
Contained within that bit of prose
That caused my admiration.

You have a certain flair, dear sir,
When a pen is in your hand.
Your thoughts flow onto paper with
An elegance quite grand!
Your humour is a wondrous thing
And your words it did enhance.
I must admit I laughed so hard
I almost wet my pants.

Do not cease to write your thoughts;
Keep pen and paper handy!
Anyone in receipt of same
Will think your letter is dandy!
I must come to conclusion now,
I'm running out of time!
The weather here is frightful cold
But Al and I are fine.

Love, Della

THE MAN WHO PLAYED GUITAR

(For our friend Bill)

There was a man who played guitar and sang a country song
So very well that country folks would listen all day long.
Although he loved to sing and play it was not his vocation,
Plumbing was his way of making money for vacation.

He fell in love with Mexico, the sea, the food, the sun,
And yearly made a trek down south, to have a little fun.
He made some friends, sipped some suds, and relaxed by the pool.
He went to bed quite early and got up the same, by rule.

Then one year he decided his guitar should come along,
And at the bar he took it out and sang a little song;
Well people hooted, yelled and cheered and party-time became
The greatest time that everyone around could even name!

The locals and the tourists came in hordes and gathered round,
Because the man who played guitar had a mesmerizing sound.
Even the Owner of the Bar, who usually closed at 10,
Stayed there and poured the many drinks
until, I don't know when!

So every day and every night our country man did sing.
They liked his song, they liked his style, they liked everything!
Soon, there was no choice except to relocate down there.
He left us all (except Collette) here in the frigid air.

He gave up plumbing; for success had made him change his trade.
Each night his old guitar case was full of pesos he had made.
He didn't have to buy his drink, 'twas provided by the crowd.
He ate for free, and by the sea, two hammocks were allowed.

Sometimes before he drifted off to sleep he'd think of those
He left behind in ice and snow (and he chuckled, I suppose).
And we, the folks he left behind, must muster from a-far
Though winter's blast and cuss a bit, the man who played guitar.

WHAT WE FOUND AT OUR HOUSE
AFTER TRAVELLING FROM BC JAN 9, 2004

Four wicked-looking guys were playing poker;
They'd finished all the wine and half the rum.
They were smoking cigarillos and a ci-gar,
We wondered where the heck they'd all come from.
A monkey (drunk) was hanging from the light fan,
In the freezer was a frozen ice-cube duck,
A little bear we saved (inside the microwave)
Who'd surely thought that he'd run out of luck!

The party had extended to our bedroom;
Under cover was a bunny and eight bears.
Another drunk was hanging from the light fan;
There was chaos and disorder everywhere!
A wee abandoned baby was discovered
From way down in the sheets (we pulled it up)
But we went into full shock, couldn't even talk,
To see a Monster Coho Salmon in our tub!

It took a while to get the house in order,
To gather up the slop and the debris.
We know for sure that when we go a travelling.
CJ will not be Keeper of the Key!
We also found a lizard in the coffee
It filled our hearts with horror and disgust.
What else is hidden there (of which we aren't aware)?
Is there no one in this world that we can trust?

THE LATEST ADDITION - FEBRUARY 08

(For our friend Sharon Hart)

Tex went into her back-room
In horror did she find
Her guitars were in a frenzy
Of a romantic kind.

She tried to separate them
But 'twas too late, it's true!
A baby Martin soon appeared
T'was brightly coloured too.

They decided to get married
To make the baby legal;
The bride wore brand new Martin strings.
The groom looked more than Regal.

The old guitars and the mandolin
Stood up while vows were spoken.
"Let not this union be untwined
Lest harmonies be broken"

Then Baby Martin played a tune
To start the celebration.
The groom then struck a sexy chord
Which caused a big sensation!

The bride, she blushed, and said to him
"If we want to stay in tune,
Before more wee ones we create
You must find us a BIGGER ROOM"!

WARNING

(Remembering that special evening Sharon
and I spent with "Jack")

Just one drink of Yukon Jack
Throws balance slightly out of whack.
Drink two and words will bungle up
Cause yer tang gets toungled up.
Yer nose gets red, yer ears get redder;
Another drink is even better
Cause that is when the giggles start,
So do be careful, Sharon Hart!

OLD FRIENDSHIPS RENEWED

(for my Pine Lake Friends and the Esso Lab Girls)

I've just renewed acquaintance
With some friends from long ago.
Those yesterdays came flooding back
Like springtime rivers flow.

What times we had, what fun we shared,
We worked but also played,
And laughter was the catalyst
That lifetime friendships made.

Though our paths went different ways
There must have been a part
Of each of them that stayed with me
Right here in my heart.

I'd forgotten what they meant to me,
These dear old friends of mine.
Now our friendship shines again.
Thank you, Father Time.

DEAR DAUGHTER

(Composed for Carol, to send to her daughter)

You know how much I love to sew; you've seen the work I do.
I'm trying to sew your Christmas gift; it will look great on you!

But someone's taking up my time (an uninvited guest),
His name is Arthur-i-tis and he's put me to the test.

He insists my dear, on holding hands, at least he's holding mine
And making it impossible to sew at all (at times).

So please be patient with me and pray Arthur goes away.
If you don't get your gift at Christmas,
I'll send it for your birthday.

But in the meantime, girl of mine, I thank the Lord above
For giving me the gift of YOU! I send you all my love.

LYNNSAY

(Granddaughter)

Born with a smile
Sweetness and light
Charming and loving
Exceptionally bright
She skipped through the years
She skipped awfully fast
For time slips away
Can't hold to the past
Girl grown to woman
Career-bound and clever
As sweet and as charming
And lovely as ever.

ODE TO THE FISHING HUT

(Inspired by Mark Dickie's story)

Once there was a fishing hut
The nicest ever built,
Well-constructed, solid, strong
And stocked right to the hilt!

It sat upon a frozen lake
Inside it was so neat,
Comfy chairs for lazy butts
To sit while hooking treats.

Pots and pans to cook the fish
And Scotch to drink as well.
All in all, this fishing hut
Was "absolutely swell!"

We know a man who was so proud
To own a hut like this.
His name was Mark and don't forget
How much he loved to fish.

One day he asked some buddies
To join him to partake
In sitting down, drinking scotch,
And fishing in the lake.

While pouring out a second scotch,
They sat around and grinned,
But just outside the weather changed
And up came a powerful wind.

Inside the hut they realized
The hut was now in motion,
They were being swept along
Like a raft upon the ocean.

This had to be the very worst
Of luck they'd had in winters.
With a crash, his precious hut
Was now a pile of splinters.

The moral of the story is:
If a great hut you have found,
Make sure you buy some long, long spikes
To fasten the darn thing down.

UP IS NOW DOWN AND DOWN IS NOW UP

(For our oldest grandson)

Jordon had a crop of curls
Red as a shiny new penny,
Where once there was this mop on top
Today there isn't any.

"Why crop your hair so close, dear boy?"
He looked at me and grinned,
"I much prefer this mop of red
That's growing from my chin."

What happened to that little boy
Who snuggled on our laps?
They must have fed him vitamins
Or growing pills, perhaps.

We used to bend to comb his curls
When they were all a-muss.
Now he stands so very tall and
Looks way down at us.

"SOMEDAY" SAID DONALEE

(I had to write a poem about my cousin's B&B preparations.)

While I renovate the room upstairs,
Upstairs has now moved down,
And mixed with all the downstairs stuff
So it's hard to get around.

My clothes are spread from here to there
Cause my closet's out of sight.
There's not a room that isn't packed,
It really is a fright!

There's just one tiny little path
From my bedroom to the loo.
I must sit sideways on the john
Cause there's furniture there too!

I'm up and down, and down and up,
I lay new floor, I paint;
And then I ache and ache some more
And feel like I might faint.

I cannot cook a simple meal,
Too much is in my way.
One problem then another;
But I survive from day to day.

So please don't come to visit me
Until I'm done upstairs
Or you'll have to sit upon the stove,
Cause there's stuff piled on the chairs.

Someday I'll have a B&B that's known the whole-world wide
Then you can come to visit me - it'll be beautiful inside!

B&B WAKE UP

(Al made a dinner gong for cousin Donalee's B&B)

When your Bed and Breakfast guests
are sleeping very sound
And you've cooked a mighty breakfast
but there's nobody around...
This little tool will help, my dear,
just strike the iron gong;
Your sleeping guests will hit the floor
and join you before long !

THE HIBERNATING BEAR

(For our friend Ken)

Within Calgary city limits,
I have a friend named Ken,
A very pleasant man is he,
and a genuine gentleman.

During summer's warmest days,
he wears a happy smile.
All summer long he gardens
and his roses bloom the while.

So when the weather turns to frost
and roses fade away,
Ken goes inside his humble home
and just plain "hides away".

He hibernates all winter
as the ice and wind and snow
cover white the countryside;
so to him I send my shows.

Gorgeous scenes of mountains white
and blue shadows on the trail,
But in trying to impress him
I very sadly fail.

I think he sits and watches
summer photos on the web,
As tropic isles and deep blue seas
are running through his head.

There's not a thing that I can do
to make him step outside
Into the world of winter
from which he tends to hide!

But I'll keep sending pictures
of the winter scenes out there,
And I know that warmth of spring
will wake the hibernating bear.

MY HUSBAND AL

My husband has the biggest heart
of anyone I know;
He feels the pain that others feel
and his tears begin to flow.
He is not weak – he's very strong –
he's every inch a man!
Who can claim to love him most?
I, for certain, can!

(Our Granddaughter, Robin, in Ontario, was to be talking on KJKL radio about what Christmas time means to her so, given advanced notice, we were waiting [and waiting)] on line.)

A POEM WHILE WAITING

Our computer has picked up your station
CJKL – Kirkland Lake,
We are waiting for something quite special
But don't know how long we must wait.

As we know, we must listen each second:
The music's not bad; 60's rock,
But we also must listen to all of the ads
While waiting for Robin to talk.

Don't forget now to order your turkey
From Clod's Meat Market today.
Kirkland Pharmacy will sell chocolate candy
And wrap them for no extra pay.

Our recorder is ready so we can record
"What Christmas Time Means To Me".
When will they play it, how long must we sit?
When we hear it, how neat it will be!

Try Dorothy's Flowers, and Fern's Restaurant
(you cannot go wrong if you go there).
Split Ends (the Hair Shop) will fix your old style,
And at the Jewel Box, a sale of their giftware.

Now for the news… sounds just the same
As the news that we listen to here.
Oh no, the next hour they will play modern POP.
We can't even plug our poor ears.

Your weather forecast: very cloudy today
With cold and some more blowing snow.
Tomorrow, a chance of flurries, and then
the same thing on Sunday you know…

Oh, next hour the music is Country
Which makes us feel somewhat relieved;
It's not country classics, but better than pop
Which is something we really don't need!

Great deals at Canadian Tire!
The Hobby shop will eliminate stress.
Northshore Outfitters has such great apparel;
Their 'Dickie' brand really is best.

We've been sitting here listening' for hours,
Here we'll stay (even though we do curse it)
But if we can tape Robin's radio voice
It all, every bit, will be worth it!

We've just heard from the radio station
Our waiting (I guess) was in vain;
Robin won't be on the air waves today
So we'll have to repeat this again!

A PUNNY POEM

(For my Punster friends)

Puns can sometimes be so strange
The cowboy got fired – now he's deranged

I watched a horror show last night
Mummies are bound to be uptight

If you knock a grape right off the vine
And you step on it – it'll give a wee whine

You want to clone yourself? You do?
Now wouldn't that be just like you.

Dogs are nice but turtles are better
My pet turtle wears people-neck sweaters

Diets are made for the short or the tall
Who really are thick and tired of it all

The making of beer just never stops
Australian beer is from Kangaroo hops

He'll hit a tree because he intends
To find out how a Mercedes bends

From Hong Kong to old Yellowknife
Stir fry cooks come from all woks of life

He hates his job, he shows the strife
But selling used cars is his lot in life

Pets are loveable – I'm sure you'll agree
My leech is very attached to me

Most annoying insects are real survivors
A mosquito is the oldest known skin-diver

I'm reading a book about anti-gravity –
And I can't seem to put it down, you see

Pandemonium is a house with veranda
Made only for Australian Pandas

At the Beanery they became inflatuated
And everyone there was evacuated

I relish the fact that you mustard the strength
to catchup to me on my punny-poem length

Thank you for having some fun-fun-fun
With a Punster and some puns-puns-puns!

RAISING BOYS

Raising little boys
can sometimes be a chore,
But there are times you wonder how
you could possibly love them more!
When wrestling with each other or
playing with their toys
you surely know you can expect
an awful lot of noise;
But when the house is quiet
but no one is asleep…
you'd better find out where they are
and take a little peek.
There's not a nicer feeling
when the day is almost done
than to have them climb upon your lap
so you can snuggle with your sons.

The teenaged years are hardest;
sons are always on your mind,
Although you love them very much
they don't return in kind.
They're learning independency
like others of their peers
and they prefer to be with friends.
They make that very clear!
Then one day, they are adults,
just overnight it seems, and
they become again the loving sons
you've longed for in your dreams.

Too big to climb upon your lap,
your heart they still can touch;
"Hi Mom — just called to tell you that
I love you very much."

EFFECTS OF THE CHINOOK

(For all those who suffer through Chinook
effects in Southern Alberta)

Don't have to look outside
There's trouble I can tell
The pressure's changing fast
I really feel like hell
Can't watch a TV show
Can't even read a book
Just lay here in the dark
And curse this damned Chinook

I've taken Tylenol
I've taken Percocet
My head is in a vise
Cause they're not working yet
Why don't I get relief
From all the pills I took
Now I am going to barf
Thanks to this damned Chinook

How slow the minutes go
It even hurts to blink
Can't even go to sleep
All I can do is think
I'm going to move up North
And live with old Nanook
Where I won't ever see
Another damned Chinook!

AN ICE FISHING STORY

T'was a fine winter's day when Eddie and Ralph
took off for a day of ice fishin',
With a thermos of soup, a bottle of rye,
and a fry-pan to cook all their fish in.
Ed's new SUV, shiny and black,
helped them travel the miles a lot faster.
His old dog lay sleeping, out-stretched in the back,
just happy to be with his Master.

The lake was a wonder, all pristine and white –
Ed drove out a ways on the ice.
The sunshine was bright; they both had a drink,
and agreed that the place was real nice!
They set up their chairs, got their poles and their hooks,
then started to drill with the auger.
Each man took his turn as the minutes flew by –
but the ice was too thick to reach water.

Now Ed was a thinker, 'No problem' he thought,
'I know how to fix this real quick'.
In the new SUV he happened to have
a most innocent dynamite stick.
No people around, so they lit the fine fuse
and Ed pitched it as far as he could.
He forgot one small thing; his Lab ran to Fetch
as any good Retriever should!

They yelled and they shrieked but the dog grabbed the stick
and trotted toward them with pride.
Ed grabbed up the rifle he'd brought "just in case"
and he aimed it just off the dog's side...

BLAM went the gun, but the dog kept his pace...
once more, and much closer, Ed fired...
This startled the dog and he headed for cover
alongside the SUV tires.

The men started running, the dog followed too;
they ran for all three of their sakes!
A mighty explosion trembled the air
and the SUV... sunk in the lake.
You may think this story's a little far-fetched,
but I tell you, my friend, it is true!
And you wouldn't be laughing at poor Ed's mistake,
if the SUV belonged to you.

TRAVIS

(Grandson)

It's most amazing, and so is he;
This child who sat upon our knees
Is growing tall and is full of fun.
He is everybody's ray of sun.

Our Grandson, who is now a teen,
Has the biggest smile I've ever seen.
He's lively, bright and seldom sad,
A replicate of his dear Dad.

I think, in all the years to come,
That life won't change this boy of fun.
Whatever he wants to be, he'll be it!
I sure hope I am around to see it.

(A poem inspired by my friend, Marilynn who told about clearing out a storage shed on the old family farm.)

MY OLD HIDDEN THINGS

(To the tune of My Favourite Things)

Old cardboard boxes and yards of old cable
Bags of some powder without any label
Parts of old chairs that need assemba-ling
These are a few of my old hidden things

Tins of hard glue and some old turpentine
Four old dead toasters that used to work fine
Ancient grass seed and some sulphur that stinks
These are a few of my old hidden things

Heavy dumbbells, sheets of cardboard,
Cans of solid paint
A really big coffin-sized old wooden box
Full of old Arbourite ... so quaint

Used furnace filters, an old mop and pail
One ancient sump pump (that might even bail)
Fluorescent lights that have no twinkle-ing
These are a few of my old hidden things

Electric heaters that actually wo-rk
Two big old pictures that could be historic
Old wooden frames good for kin-dle-ing
These are some more of my old hidden things

An old blow torch, sheets of metal,
Old fridge shelves and drawers
This is just one of the places I've purged
And I have to clean out TWO more!!!!!

I'M PLAYING SECOND
FIDDLE TO A BANJO

(a song for our friend Eva and in memory of Roy Dickie)

I met a man in Castlegar, a charming man was he.
Soon we were a-courting and I was on his knee.
The love I thought was heaven-sent is filling me with doubt,
Cause when I want a little squeeze he pulls his banjo out.

I'm playing second fiddle to a banjo.
I think he might be stringing me along.
I know that I am not his one and only,
Cause he wants to pluck his banjo all night long.

I went to a department store, a nightie I did buy,
Very black and slinky and sure to catch his eye.
When he saw me in it, he said "I'll be with you soon,
Right now I'm awful busy cause my banjo's out of tune."

Though I try to tune him in, I'm getting mighty sore;
I get a little loving but the banjo gets much more.
I'm starting to resent the fact that I am number two.
I wish to heck the banjo jokes they tell would all come true!

(i.e., What do you do if you drive over a banjo? Back up!)

THE ONLY KIND OF PET I'LL EVER OWN

My little dust bunnies (Sissy, Moe 'n Fluffy)
Little dust bunnies (Ringo, Sam an' Tuffy)
They're so cute and soft and shy; they roll out when I walk by.
Don't have to feed them, still they keep on growing.
I can leave them, no matter where I'm going.
They're prolific, to be specific, but the
only kind of pet I'll ever own.

Dogs are great but then you have to feed them;
And the cost of Puppy Chow is getting high.
Cats are kind of fun but they need their freedom
And they'll never be your friend although you try.
A hamster is a hamster – they'd rather sleep than play,
My bunnies are the best pets – they hide 'n seek all day.

Birds are good companions if you're lonely
But their noise can be annoying to the ear
A ferret likes to play but it is only
A smelly little critter when it's near
Fish are very pretty, but all they do is swim!
But bunnies make me laugh out loud
when things are looking' grim.

They never lap up water in the bathroom,
They never need a tether, cage or pen.
Every now and then I use the vacuum
But my little bunnies all come back again.
They don't chew on my furniture, they never make a fuss,
And robbers won't break in my house out of pure disgust!

THE WAREHOUSE STORE

(A little ditty for those who shop at the big warehouse stores)

I should have stayed at home today and not gone out the door.
Everything that could go wrong went wrong and that's for sure!
I've never, ever, had a rotten day like this before.
Today I lost my Sweetie in the Warehouse Store

Boxes reaching to the ceiling, miles of aisles, each one revealing
Stock so thick that no one can see through.
One moment he was standing there, then he was gone, I don't know
where.
I've searched and searched! Oh gosh, what can I do?

I wandered up and down those aisles full of goods galore,
So I did a little shopping, then I did a whole bunch more!
All the while I called his name although it was a chore.
Today I lost my Sweetie in the Warehouse Store

At last I found a Lost and Found - my hopes began to soar,
But all they had were 14 kids and a parakeet that swore.
I think he's really gone for good. I won't see him no more.
Today I lost my Sweetie in the Warehouse Store.

OH, BROTHER! WHERE AM I?

(Inspired by friends in Songsmiths Ink)

The Calgary of my childhood was simple in design
With numbered streets and avenues displayed on corner signs.
If there really was a Place Name you knew where it would be;
Centre Street was Centre Street...but things changed drastically...

Now people live on a Green or a Mews or a Place
Or a Rise or a Ranch or a Way,
Some folks live on a Close or a Gate or a Park
or a Cove or an Island, or Parade.

They reside on a Grove, or a Terrace or a Ridge
or a Hollow or a Key or a Link,
There are those on a Bend, on a Cape, on a Court,
Things are getting really weird don't you think?

There are Paths, there are Lanes, even Walks, there are Hills,
there are Heights, there are Vistas, there are Views.
There are Gardens, there are Villas, also there are Bays.
Our City Planners need to have a talking-to!

People live on a Pointe, or a Manor, or a Heath
Or a Landing or a Circle or a Square,
Or a Common or a Haven or a Row or a Woods -
It's a wonder we can find Anywhere!

MY WONDERFUL OLD SOCKS

(For Eva)

I have a pair of knitted socks
Made by Eva's hands
Two-toned blue with stripes around
In little narrow bands
She gave these socks to me one day
For no apparent reason
With just a wish that they would keep
Me warm through winter's season

When the snow began to fall
And winter winds did blow
The temperature was dropping down
To 30 C below
I crawled into my comfy bed
It felt so warm and sweet
Because I had those knitted socks
Upon my thankful feet

For many winter's now they've helped
To keep me warm as mink
The heels developed two big holes
I've mended them with pink
They're looking much the worse for wear
But when I put them on
I may not be too stylish but
My feet are warm till dawn!

MY CUP OF JOY

(For Stephen, Jamie, Doug and Shawn)

My cup of joy would be more joyful
if my house were not so boy full.
That is what I used to say
Way back in those ol' by-gone days.
I take it back, I miss the noise
Created by my little boys!
It took some time to realize
They were miracles before my eyes.
After all is said and done,
My cup of joy is still my sons.

HANNAH

(Granddaughter)

You'd have thought she was a baby doll;
that new-born preemie, so very small.
A wee, heart-warming, precious sight
but God gave her the will to fight;

and fight she did as years went by.
At times her battles multiplied,
but love enough from Mom and Dad
helped conquer struggles that she had.

Today, almost a woman grown,
achievements are her very own.
My heart, dear Hannah, you beguile.
I'll love you always, dear grandchild.

THE
CONTINUING SAGAS

THE GAFFLEBITER JOURNALS

(It all started when I emailed my friend, Marilynn Stratton, and told her about a group of local musicians called the Gafflebiters.)

Marilynn replied, "I'd like to know what the heck a gaffle is, and what it tastes like when it's bitten. I assume you don't bite a gaffle unless it's already dead or heavily sedated. I mean, what if it wasn't and it bit back? Are you supposed to bite them cooked or raw? Inquiring minds want to know.)

The following was my reply. "Here's a description of the Gafflebiter, but it's up to you to describe the Gaffle."

BEWARE THE GAFFLEBITER

Beware the Gafflebiter, friend,
With razor teeth at either end.
On chunks of Gaffle it depends
(And Gaffles take some time to mend).

The Gafflebiter's quite diverse.
It also gallops in reverse,
Coming or going it's such a curse.
It's never bit humans – don't want to be first!

The Gafflebiter looks a fright;
Its teeth are red its eyes are white,
It sleeps by day and roams by night
Hunting Gaffles, just to bite.

So if you ever chance upon
A Gafflebiter on your lawn,
Keep your bedroom curtains drawn
Cause it will stay from dusk to dawn.

Once it's gone I'm sure you'll find
A very messy scene behind,
But open up and do be kind -
Bandage the Gaffles on which it dined.

Marilynn replied as follows:

REGARDING GAFFLE,

You asked me to describe a Gaffle
But I've not seen it -- I'm all a'baffle?
I know it's shorter than a giraffle
(probably at least by halfle?),
And it's easy to bite, so NOT made of taffle?
And it's not a shishkabob, nor a falaffel?
And I've never won one in a raffle
Nor have I ever heard it laffle?

So -- since I've no ideas here
And with my time I MUST be frugal,
Decided to get help, my dear
And simply looked it up on Google!
And there it was, just zippity-ZAP.
An actual WORD, from the world of rap.
A VERB it is, they define "to gaffle"
It means to swipe, or steal, or snaffle.

So if we convert it to a noun
A Gaffle's visit will make you frown.

It'll steal your doorknobs and swipe your shoes
And everything you own, you'll LOSE.
And the ONLY thing that stops the blighters
Is that nightly herd of Gaffle-Biters!

To which I replied:
Brilliant (I can even detect Ogden Nash (giraffle? laffle?)
Aren't we clever? Aren't we great? We're absolutely First Rate!
We should combine our talents and write a book of poetry
entitled "What Came First, the Gaffle or the Gafflesbitter?" Della

And then came this one....

Della -- maybe, if you asked a Gafflebiter how a Gaffle tastes,
it would say "bitter" and make a vile "it's SO bitter" face, which
also probably accounts for why the Gafflebiters only bite and don't
actually EAT the bitter Gaffles which, of course, leads me down
another tangential train of thought entirely, and that would be to
question the intelligence of the Gafflebiters?
They must be terribly slow learners to keep ON biting the Gaffles
when the last seventeen hundred and forty six Gaffles they bit
were too bitter to eat -- wouldn't you THINK the Gafflebiters
would STOP biting bitter Gaffles and turn their attentions
elsewhere? So either, the Gafflebiters aren't too bright -- or
they all suffer from serious (and obviously hereditary) obsessive-
compulsive disorder which manifests itself in the overwhelming
and compulsive need to bite every Gaffle they see, even though they
know full well that Gaffles are too bitter to eat? Marilynn

So, I lay abed that evening with Gaffle garble running
through my head and had to climb out of bed early the
next morning to write the following which had been
already composed in my Gaffle-filled night dreams:

Do Gaffles gobble garbage
Or do Gaffles gobble grass?

Whatever Gaffles gobble
It gives them awful gas.

Gaffle gas is gruesome.
After gobbling a plateful,
Oh my goodness gracious,
Give them Tums and they'll be grateful!

THE GREETING CARD JOURNAL

(Judy Dundas, an old friend of mine, has my crazy sense of humour. When I found a greeting card that said "If a chicken and a half laid an egg and a half in a day and a half, then how long would it take a grasshopper with a wooden leg to kick all the seeds out of a dill pickle?", I knew Judy would love it. She did and she kept it for a few years and then sent it back to me, and I did the same thing, so that card went back and forth many times. Judy once sent a note in it, asking some questions about the characters in the card. I answered as follows.)

Dear Judy, thank you for your note
In which you asked… now let me quote,

"Why does the grasshopper have a wooden leg?
What colour was the chicken's egg?
What style of pickle was the dill?
What chicken half survived the kill?
What age is each of the above?
What race is the 'How Long' made of?"
After many years of card reflection
You're asking me such silly questions
But I will try to do my best
To put your active mind at rest.
So here we go, pull up a chair
Cause something tells me you'll be there
For quite a while as I enlighten
You with facts that just might frighten!

Let's start with Hoppy – that's his name
Of Olympic Pickle-Kicking fame
T'was during a triathlon,
An olive he did stumble on.
He fell real hard and broke his leg

But grabbed a toothpick as a peg
And carried on and won the race;
The toothpick was his saving grace.

About the chicken's egg and hue,
They laid not white or brown, but blue.
This happened after Farmer Taff
Chopped a chicken quite in half
To let the other chickens know
The egg productions gotta grow!
If his request they couldn't meet,
He'd split their personalities.
They felt depressed (you'd be too)
That's why the eggs they laid were blue.
The half-a-chicken didn't dare
To croak and die so did its share;
Each half a chick laid half an egg.
Please sympathize with them, I beg.

What kind of pickle was the dill?
As I recall, with quite a thrill,
It was so very large and green
The largest Garlic Dill I've seen.
It cracked the jar and then sprung loose
And on the table lay the juice
So it would take a Star, at least
To kick the seeds out of this Beast.
He'd have to hop upon the table
Then swim as fast as he was able,
Then kick till all the seeds were gone –
Someone who knows 'Triathalon".
TA DA! We know who that would be!
It's just as clear as clear can be.

What age the Hopper and the Chick?
What age the slender toothy-pick?
I can tell you just 'How Long'
Has been around, but I'd be wrong,
So off a-pondering I will go
Because I simply do not know.

If you can shed some light some day
About this problem, please, do say!
To answer now, your query re:
Is 'How Long' a Vietnamese?
Or is he Chinese or Korean?
None of these, this human bein'
Fits our own Canadian bill
Remember his name? 'How Long **Will**'.

I hope your curiosity
Feels no animosity
About the facts I'm telling you
And every one I swear is true.
You are such a special friend.
Thanks for being you. The End.

*(Then came the day when the chicken fell off the card, who
knows where, which prompted me to reply to Judy as follows.)*

For years she was our faithful pet
And guarded our old card.
Back and forth that card did go
Her job was very hard.

When you told me she was missing
I shed a little tear.
The only thing that we can do
Is just 'surmise', my dear.

Could it be she ran away
To adorn some modern greeting?
Maybe she was too ashamed
Cause our card sure took a beating.

She might have been quite lonely
So went looking for a Cock,
But she might have caught the bird flu
Or come down with Chicken Pox.

Or maybe she was just plain bored
And needed an adventure.
Let's hope she didn't hurt herself
With some highly dangerous venture.

Or maybe she went looking
For her infamous 'half' sister
(the one who laid a half an egg)
Because she really missed her.

Perhaps she joined a group of folk
Who drank more than a few
And they sat her on a can of beer
On someone's bar-be-que.

She might have found a Chicken Spa
When she flew the chicken coop;
The hot tub might have been too hot
And now she's Chicken Soup.

But could it be… yes, yes, I'm sure!
That she was old and tired
And has given up her job
To join those who've retired.

So now we have to let her go
And find another chicken.
I'm sending applications.
Please, Judy, do the pickin'.

CARD FRONT CHICKEN REQUIRED

Qualifications:

1. Must be able to stand quietly for long periods of time
2. Must be ready to travel at any given moment
3. Must be patient with invalid grasshoppers
4. Must like dill seeds
5. Minimal salary, but all the laughter you can stomach.

JOB APPLICATION #1

Name: **Henrietta Hen**
Age: *Spring Chicken*
Experience: *Folks tell me I'm quite a card*

JOB APPLICATION #2

Name: **Chick-a-Boom**
Age: *Forever young*
Experience: *My musical talent prevents boredom while fronting cards*

JOB APPLICATION #3

Name: **Cocky**
Age: Young *and virile*
Experience: *I've never laid an egg, let alone an egg-and-a-half but I've laid lots of chickens!*

GIVING THANKS

THANK YOU DEAR FATHER

Thank you, dear Father; I thank you so much
For the beauty this day I could see and could touch;
Fields of wildflowers in a mass of bright shades,
Their glorious fragrance was heavenly made.
Those fast moving clouds in a brilliant blue sky,
Kept changing the picture as they swiftly flew by.
How lucky I am to have sight and can view
The beauty of nature created by you.

(This poem was inspired by
a story of the same name, author-unknown)

A LITTLE CHILD WHISPERED

A little child whispered "God, speak to me"
And a nightingale sang its sweet melody
But the child did not hear and the child wondered why
God had not spoken, so he yelled to the sky,
"God, let me see you – please show me you care."
A small brilliant rainbow answered his prayer.
The child did not notice and in a voice loud and clear,
"Dear Father, please touch me and show me you're here."
When a butterfly landed upon his small hand
He brushed it away. He did not understand.
We are no longer children and still there are times
We don't hear His voice or see His stars shine.
Let us take time to listen – take time to see
All the blessings He's granting to you and to me.

CPSIA information can be obtained
at www.ICGtesting.com
Printed in the USA
BVHW070544260121
598716BV00010B/73

9 781460 267752